GOOSE ON THE GREEN

A Kitchen Garden Book

Text © Francine Raymond
Illustrations © Gabrielle Stoddart

By the same Author.
In the same series:
Food from the Kitchen Garden
Beekeeping for Beginners (with P. Hands)
Keeping a few Ducks in your Garden
A Peacock on the Lawn (with S. Carpenter)
Also:
The Big Book of Garden Hens
A Henkeeper's Journal
A Christmas Journal

Published by the Kitchen Garden 2005
Troston
Suffolk 1P31 1EX
Tel 01359 268 322
Email: francine@jfraymond.demon.co.uk
www.kitchen-garden-hens.co.uk

ISBN 0-9532857-8-2

Printed in England on recycled paper

Many thanks to: Hugh Burton, Jane Breach,
Penelope Hands, Jacqui Collier, Mike Hall, Sue Carpenter,
Jo Kendall and Hester Page.

'Man has wisely selected the Goose from the number of feathered tribes that once roamed at large, and by domestication has made him a source of real wealth.'

Montague's Ornithological Dictionary of British Birds 1831.

Introduction

Geese are not backyard poultry. They are more at home on smallholdings, in paddocks and orchards, so an acre at least and access to water are a must before considering these beguiling creatures. Once a common sight; the sentinels at every farm gate, I still pass one small flock regularly and it cheers me to see them - gander with defiant head held high - daring me to approach, and his wives, busily grazing their patch of grass.

Producers of gargantuan grade A eggs, and premium home-reared meat, geese supply top-grade fertilizer, soil conditioner and compost activator. They are maintenance-free lawn mowers and land grazers, honking a strident alarm audible to the entire neighbourhood, and they'll entertain the whole family (though I would never totally trust a goose with small children). Geese are so easy to keep, but you need space, and above all you need commitment.

Sadly, I haven't the sort of acreage sufficient to entertain even a pair. But the stories that each of my sources tell about their charges make me long to feel the affinity only a goose owner experiences. Goose people really love their geese. So, I shall have to comfort myself with reporting the facts, and while encouraging you to keep them, perhaps I can live vicariously through your adventures.

Waterfowl are hardier than other poultry, less prone to infection, longer-lived and they lay longer. My friend Jane Breach, a committed goose keeper, says she has never known a sick goose, or a silly one for that matter - they are highly intelligent. So, unless you are going to eat them, a goose really is for life - not just for Christmas.

Where to Begin

First, check with your Town Hall's Environmental Health Department, and with your neighbours. I'm afraid your honking flock will alert the whole county and make them aware of any comings or goings - a sort of avian Neighbourhood Watch.

Geese are the cheapest of lodgers, but the larger breeds are expensive to buy, especially the ornamentals, so stick to the smaller utility strains suggested in the Breeds section. Start with a pair of ladies or - if you have space and confidence - a gander and two unrelated geese.

Finding your first gaggle will be fun. Visit local poultry shows, charm waterfowl-keeping friends for their surplus stock, and scan the smallholder magazines for breeders. The Domestic Waterfowl Club (see Directory) will recommend, but always inspect stock, ordering well beforehand, and have your pen, shelter and feed ready and waiting when you collect in early winter. Pairing starts in early autumn, so check your pair are, in fact, a pair.

Adopt a routine that suits you both. Your flock should be fed in the morning in the pen, let out to graze, potter, preen and doze till sunset, then encouraged back to their quarters for supper and bed. Jane Breach lets her Embden crosses live a natural life, unpenned on her four-acre smallholding with a pond. She loses the odd one to the dog fox, but feels that's a small price to pay for their freedom. Grazing mostly at night, one gander is always on guard and gives the alarm. A few straw bales are all the shelter needed during the worst winter months.

My good friend Penelope Hands discovered she was entitled to keep a pair of geese on the village green in her house deeds, as are her neighbours. Consulting her Parish Council, she has kept a few birds on the village duckpond ever since. Sleeping and nesting on an island in the pond, occasionally there are complaints; wheelchairs bogged down in goose mess, ruined Italian sandals, gander attacks on cars and sometimes the local butcher has to deal with their prolific offspring. Penny is a passionate goosekeeper, much preferring them to her hens and ducks.

Finally, though these birds are hardy, easy and great fun to keep, remember you'll have to clean out their shelter regularly and visit them every day - though the temptation will be to spend much longer watching their antics - all poultry are great time wasters. Geese live many years, so adopting a flock can be quite a commitment, but long term connections can be hugely fulfilling. How I envy you.

Where to Keep Your Geese
Geese see in the dark and doze with one eye and half their brain alert to predators, but you'll still have to protect your flock against foxes and uncontrolled dogs, especially if they can't fly because they are jumbo sized or have clipped wings.

Their ideal home is a shed or shelter in the middle of a netted pen, leading to a paddock, field or orchard with a pond or riverbank. Keep them penned for the first few weeks, till they know their address. Be warned, geese are master escapologists so smaller breeds may need the first few flight feathers on one wing trimmed. Ask your breeder to do this. All waterfowl prefer moving water, so the area right down to the riverbed should be netted with galvanized wire to stop your flock sailing away. Visiting wildfowl are always a nuisance and will inter-breed and steal food.

People will tell you it's possible to keep geese without a pond, and although they're not as aquatic as ducks, it would be hard to deny them a small pond at least. They love to paddle in and out of the water, and preen, and some of the larger breeds like the extra buoyancy for successful mating. Though seeming content in the most appalling conditions, (a small flock has set up home locally in a disused swimming pool), allow the largest pond possible, bearing in mind, even shallow water can be dangerous to small children.

Concrete or simple fibreglass ponds of a foot depth in the middle with gradated access, can be cleaned with a broom and hose run to overflow. The Domestic Fowl Trust supplies a mail order pond (see Directory). If you are excavating a pond, use a strong butyl liner and fold sturdy plastic netting round the turf edges to stop the perimeter being dabbled away. Alternatively protect banks with flints, logs or flagstones angled with a camber. Water levels will probably need topping up during periods of drought.

If you live in a very foxy area, perhaps you should think again. You could build a pen with a netted roof and cut away overhanging branches of nearby trees, making use of one of the electric fences advertised in the poultry press, but a determined fox will include you as part of his daily routine and visit every day until you forget to shut the pen. I have even heard of foxes circling pens for hours on end and worrying geese to death.

Geese are very hardy. House them for protection and easy egg collection rather than night time comfort. They need shelter of about a square metre per bird, with a large door. Unlike other poultry, geese are wary of popholes and won't go in to sleep or lay. They don't roost, so above head height is useful only to you for easy access mucking-out. If you have to crouch, you'll be less inclined to carry out your housekeeping duties.

Make sure the floor is kept dry or the occupants will develop problems with arthritis in their legs and feet and refuse to come in. Cover the floor with newspaper and then add a thick layer of straw or corrugated cardboard bedding (available from your feed merchant) and replace when damp. The sweepings will rot down nicely on the compost heap.

If your geese come to you determinedly free range and unused to being housed, then at least pen them at night in safety. You could use a large portable rigid wire pen, encouraging them in at night with a handful of corn or herding them with whippy sticks. They can be trained; think of all those fairytale goosegirls.

Which Breed

Domestic geese have evolved from the various wild species whose chevrons augur winter so magically. A few breeds were developed to lay; the white ones bred to supply feathers and down, some were bred for their beauty, but most, especially massive Toulouse were obviously destined for the table.

First evidence of domestication appears in Mesopotamian carvings dating from 2400 BC, and geese crop up regularly in Egyptian wall paintings. Both Aesop and Aristotle chronicled their husbandry, (possibly using goose quills) and in 388 BC, the Gauls' attack on Rome was prevented by goose alert - as every embryonic Latin scholar will tell you. Caesar reported that our ancestors kept geese as sacred objects rather than as a source of food, and these birds would have been the forefathers of the huge East Anglian flocks that were herded to the capital with their feet shod in tar.

Always popular on mixed farms because of their self-sufficiency, geese would fatten up on stubble grass after harvest and gobble up orchard windfalls, only to be offered as Michaelmas rent to the landowner. The rest were plumped up on grain, then driven to the Christmas markets.

A goose is the ultimate multi-purpose bird. Dorothy Hartley in her mighty tome 'Food in England' tells of goose fat being eaten on toast or whipped into a mayonnaise with lemon juice. Rubbed to get a shine on metal pots, goose grease was prescribed as a poultice for invalids, as handcream for dairymaids, as lotion for cows' udders and for babies with chapped lips. In the tackroom it was smeared on harness and leather goods, rubbed on sheepdogs' ears and paws, and anointed to highlight beaks and legs by proud poultry showmen. The curled feathers were used for fishing tackle, the flights to steady arrows by fletchers and the quills by artists; and housemaids removed dust from velvet with stiff plumes. Goosedown is the softest filling of all for pillows and duvets. Quite an inventory.

Goose was especially popular as a meat source during the war when the feeding of animals with foods fit for human consumption (including grain) was banned, and flocks could fend for themselves. I have a wartime book on geese listing enviable reprint runs during the early nineteen forties.

Starting from scratch, I suggest you buy two of the smaller breeds of geese and then hatch out a few goslings from fertile hatching eggs over the next few years, to bring the flock up to the sort of numbers your land can cope with. Keep one young gander, bearing in mind pairs mate for life and pine miserably if separated. They even need a period of mourning after the death of a partner. The heavier breeds do best in pairs or trios, but in a flock of smaller geese, one gander will manage up to six ladies.

To see a full list of domestic breeds, consult the British Poultry Standards book at your local library, but here are a good half dozen:

Embden *(Germany)*

A huge (over 30lbs/14kg) snow-white shapely bird, bred in Germany where goose is the meat of choice at Christmas. Upright, defiant and handsome, with orange beak, webs and legs- the goose of nursery rhymes. Also valued for its white down and feathers. Good mothers, laying only 20 eggs per year. Effective burglar deterrent with a strident call. Needs water to keep feathers spotless.

Toulouse *(France)*

Bruiser of the goose world, with low-slung keel and triple chin, originally bred unsurprisingly for the table. Docile with majestic ruffled bulk, but shouldn't be allowed to get too paunchy or health will suffer. Give plenty of opportunity for exercise by keeping food some distance from the pen and avoid showbird strains. Expensive, needing a stress-free environment to live a long and happy life.

Pilgrim *(GB)*

Charming bird with upright stance, seems to be standing on tiptoes. Taken to America by the Pilgrim Fathers. The gander is pure white and his lady is grey with a black/white back and a white bottom. Young are easy to sex (males yellow, females grey) and easy to raise. Docile, quiet and possibly best geese with children (15lb/7kg).

Chinese *(Asia)*

A light, stylish, shapely goose with a graceful swanlike appearance and a knob on top of its beak. Lays up to 100 eggs a year and sits well. Some strains need protection from the cold. Available in white with an orange beak or grey/brown with a black beak. The gander is especially noisy with a harsh call. Breeder Hugh Burton says the greys are particularly handsome.

Brecon Buff *(Wales)*

Medium/large sized goose (18lbs/8kg) that lays well. Bred in Wales in the 1930s, both sexes are buff coloured with nice milk chocolate markings and unusual pink accessories. Friendly, with a docile temperament, this is the best layer of the heavier birds. A good forager that does well in colder climates. Not to be confused with the American Buff - a separate breed in a paler shade of buff.

Roman *(Italy)*

A smaller, chubby, pure white goose (12lbs/6kg) introduced from Italy, but probably originally Romanian. Impressive fertility and strong maternal instincts. Neat, active and nippy, with pinkish orange legs, bill and webs. Jacqui Collier's friendly ganders feed from her hand and wake her every morning at the same time. Excellent for smaller gardens. Good value for money. A first class beginner's bird.

What to Feed your Geese

Basically geese need grass, grain, grit and water to survive. They are herbivores, (not omnivores like other forms of poultry) needing large amounts of good grazing supplemented with helpings of mixed corn. A flock works well in a mixed smallholding, grazing much shorter grass than other stock. Your gaggle will also flourish in a large orchard, finishing up windfalls. They don't thrive on really rough pasture, so when grass loses its goodness (between October and April) substitute brassicas, salads and cooked root veg with extra corn and pellets. Beware, geese mess a lot, so don't encourage backdoor snacking. Local legend tells the tale of old Mr. Pamett, a countryman who lived in squalor alone with his house goose.

Offer grain in a sturdy trough in their shelter or pen for twenty minutes when you get up and again at sunset, and leave your flock to top up with grass. If you want lots of eggs, feed 80% mixed corn to 20% goose pellets from your feed merchant. Allen and Page supply organic and GM free poultry food, recommended by the Soil Association and the Vegetarian Society (see Directory). Take care not to leave those plastic twines from feed sacks on the ground, or your geese may playfully gobble them up and harm themselves.

Galvanized feeders and drinkers are more robust than plastic alternatives, except during really icy weather, when several washing-up bowls will do the trick. Clean drinking water is absolutely essential for waterfowl. Grit, needed for digestion, is naturally available in your garden soil, but supply, if for any reason, your birds are confined. Keep your grain and pellets in galvanized dustbins with metal lids to deter rats and make sure any leftover food is put away between feeds.

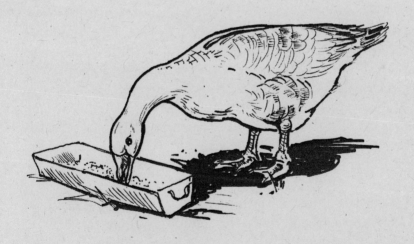

Eggs

A goose doesn't need a gander to produce eggs. Encourage her to lay by boarding the darkest end of the shelter with a large plank to provide a roomy nesting area. Fill with a thick, comfy layer of straw and add a couple of large china broody eggs. Pick up any eggs you find lying round the pen to discourage vermin.

You can take the first and second clutch of eggs for the kitchen, but geese won't supply you consistently in the way ever-obliging hens or some breeds of ducks do. You might get eighty eggs a year from Chinese Browns, but not the 300 eggs a year that Khaki Campbell ducks produce. Of course, goose eggs are much bigger, weighing in at a massive 8oz/200grams each, as opposed to hens' eggs at 65gms and duck eggs weighing up to 100gms.

Geese usually lay early in the morning every other day, starting traditionally on Valentine's Day, but realistically any time from mid-winter to mid-summer, depending on the weather. Take them fresh from the nest box for cooking if you don't want them for hatching, but take care, a goose will be very protective of her clutch, to say nothing of the gander. The first few eggs are usually infertile, but mark them and leave them *in situ* so as not to discourage her, but once you have a few more they can safely be used in the kitchen. Excellent in quiches, flans and custards, with a creamy flavour, the whites can't be whipped for meringues or soufflés.

Goose eggs are difficult to sell, but if you have a glut, contact DEFRA for their advice on sales. It's probably better to use the eggs for baking and put the cakes in the freezer. Apparently there is a good market amongst the craft fraternity who will blow and decorate goose eggs for sale.

Excess ganders are often culled to roast, especially for Christmas feasts. You'll find this very hard to contemplate - they are your friends, but it is a solution to the gander ratio problem, and having had a good life the meat will be free range and very tasty. Unlike most poultry, goosemeat has more flavour in a two or three year old bird. Candidates should be stunned and then have their throats slit. Ducks and Geese at Home by M & V Roberts (chapter - Fattening and Killing for Home Consumption) goes into this in gruesome detail, but you'll probably find your local butcher keen to come and take them - goosemeat is luxury fare.

Augmenting your Flock

Geese are xenophobic and can be extremely unwelcoming to newcomers, (though breeders say pairs of single ladies of breeding age are readily accepted in the pecking order), so the easiest way to increase your flock is to hatch. If you prefer to incubate, I suggest you read Batty's Artificial Incubation & Rearing (See Directory) but youngsters without a mum to support them will have to be segregated until they can hold their own. Hatching out your own goslings under their mum is the nicest way to build up your stock.

Place a couple of broody eggs in the nest box to encourage mum to lay. Leave her daily eggs until she has a clutch, not too many or chaos will ensue, and she'll have trouble covering more than six eggs. If you want to try a new breed or don't have a gander, or your flock needs new blood, you can buy fertile hatching eggs from a breeder. Only set eggs that are less than 7 days old and have been kept in a cool place. Reject any that are damaged, oddly shaped or unusually large or small. First time mums are often unsuccessful with their first clutch.

The goose will line her nest with down plucked from her breast - premium down, (if prices of goosefeather pillows are anything to go by) and carefully cover her eggs when she nips out to feed. Make sure she has access nearby to food and enough water to drink and immerse her head, and clear away any mess daily.

The incubation period is 30 to 32 days from the time mum starts to sit on her clutch. The goslings will take a nailbitingly long time to chip their way out of the shell. Don't be tempted to help, they will stay under their mother for two days, surviving on food from the egg. And don't be disappointed with the resulting numbers - goose eggs have a low hatching rate.

The gander will pace about outside the pen like an expectant father. He can be re-united with his family when mum leads her brood out from the nest. Goslings are gorgeous - reward her with a big feed, but be careful - both parents are fiercely protective. Other females in the flock will help to look after the young, like maiden aunts.

Feed the babes little and often on gosling crumbs, boiled rice, and chopped lettuce, and offer access to good, short grass - they'll grow like wildfire. For the first three weeks, provide water in a drinker on a netted base so they don't submerge themselves and chill. Unlike most birds, geese don't feed their young - except by enthusiastic example. They can be left to bring up their offspring without your help, but keep them in a roofed pen for a week with extra shelter, (which you may have to encourage the goslings to use in heavy downpours) and make sure later there is easy access out of the pond.

Orphans can be hand reared with lots of cuddles, warmth and attention. Pairs do best; they make wonderful pets but can't be returned to the flock until fully grown. Goslings from non colour-linked breeds are very difficult to sex. Some keepers say the only time you can be sure you've got a goose is when she lays.

Ganders can live for thirty years, and are not ready to breed until two or three years old. Bigger than their wives, with different plumage in some breeds, they are aggressive and full of bravado, standing protectively between you and their flock, hissing with neck outstretched, but they make great dads. A hiss is just a warning, but during the mating season, geese are particularly bellicose, and while offspring are being hatched, you may need to carry a stick. Please don't let young children anywhere near their pen alone at this time, and always discourage teasing.

Gardening with Geese
I must admit that geese would be my last choice as co-gardeners. I suppose a large garden could cope with a pair of Chinese or Romans, but it's important for the health and welfare of both geese and garden that you provide as much space as possible. Grass is their main source of food and they need more grazing than most gardens have to offer.

The two major problems are the trample factor - geese have big feet - and the mess, especially round the pond. Lawns can be swept clean with a besom brush or a quick burst with a high-speed hose, but I defy you to deal with large quantities of goose poo. Vulnerable areas of the garden should be fenced off to a metre high, because virtually anything that is green and sappy will be nibbled away or trampled into the ground. Young trees need their bark protected up to a metre, especially fruit trees. Be prepared, if you intend to keep your flock in the orchard.

Say goodbye to frogs, ornamental fish and any other pond wildlife. I'm not sure how many would actually be gobbled up, but any survivors will soon perish as the droppings foul the water and nitrogen levels rocket. You could excavate a decorative pond elsewhere in the garden, planted with vigorous water greenery, then covered with weldmesh panels, so wildlife could creep underneath and the plants poke through the wire.

On the upside, geese love clover (tougher grasses, docks, thistles or nettles are not on the menu) and will keep the grass down in rougher areas of the garden. They will forage ditches, hedgerows and boggy areas with minimun soil compaction and if you need a lake cleared of excess vegetation, call in your gaggle. Their droppings fertilize the soil, and bedding and feathers make excellent compost when added to the heap, layered with other kitchen and garden waste.

I've just visited Jolyon and Jemima/Jimmy, two Roman ganders who rule the roost on Jacqui Collier's pond, satisfying their paternal instincts by corraling all the Mallard ducklings long after their own drake fathers have lost interest. Be wary though, of penning your flock with other garden familiars, ducks and hens will be bullied, but on the open farm, most animals learn to avoid the belligerent elements. You can train your own dogs, but other peoples' pets are often a problem, especially with goslings. Foxes are the worst transgressors and I've had bad experiences with herons taking ducklings. All young waterfowl are vulnerable to hawks, mink, rats and stoats, but with mum, dad and aunts in tow, most predators give geese a wide berth.

Keeping poultry encourages other birds to your garden. Softest goose-down will line all their nests, and swallows will gather mud from the banks of your pond.

Problems
Geese seem to be amazingly hardy creatures, and thrive with little imput from their owners. Give them lots of space and rotate their grazing or the land will become infested with worms. Though largely resistant to parasites, if your birds are not thriving and you suspect worms, your vet or farm supplier can prescribe a remedy. A little crushed garlic in their drinking water is a good preventative.

Provide lots of clean water for drinking and preening or your birds will suffer from sore eyes. Waterfowl kept on the hard, with no opportunity to swim, can get corns and callouses on their webs and develop arthritis if their bedding is damp and left to rot. Homeopathy provides several good remedies, and massage with warm olive oil can help if you and the patient are on good terms. Isolate any lame bird in a separate coop with plenty of bedding and lots to eat and drink until she recovers. Spray-on iodine is a useful wound healing treatment.

Geese moult in the autumn and your garden will be full of pretty feathers. Never clip wings or trim feathers during the moult. All poultry are prone to lung diseases from damp bedding. Make sure yours sleep on dry straw - not hay, which can harbour fungal moulds.

In summer, check that your flock has access to shady spots, because sunstroke is not uncommon, especially if the water supply dries up as well. Isolate with plenty of both, if you notice a bird sitting with laboured breathing.

Like all poultry, geese are very difficult to catch. They always seem to know exactly what you have in mind. I craftily trap my ducks by building a large wire cage and feeding them ever nearer and then inside it. Then, I drop the door, but this takes about a week. You can catch geese in their shelter at night, but in an emergency, use a strong fish landing net. They are pretty unbiddable, but can be herded into a cage with long whippy sticks.

Ganders vary hugely and should always be approached with care. If geese accost in a threatening way, your best bet is to stand still, and then start again slowly - or beat a retreat backwards. Move unhurriedly amongst your flock, talking all the time. Watch their wings, they can cause really bad bruising and sometimes even break bones. When they nip, they twist - very painfully. A friend tells me he was bruised through a shirt, sweater and leather jacket. It can be hard to tame goslings when young, because their parents are so protective, but persevere. I've heard lots of charming stories about very friendly geese.

If you have to handle a goose, it's best to back her into a corner in the pen and grasp her by the neck at the back of the head. This isn't easy because she will always try to keep her head facing towards you. When the wings are secured, slide one hand under her breast and grasp her legs, keeping her head gently under your arm, so both the angry end and the messy end are well away from you. Use your other arm to steady the wings. Keep talking quietly, and remember - panic breeds panic. If you need to transport geese, pop them in a big, strong, ventilated cardboard box or dog cage, lined with lots of newspaper, and place on the back seat of the car, rather than in an airless boot, because they quickly overheat.

Rats are the poultry keeper's number one enemy. Deter them by keeping all feed in bins and clearing away any leftovers. Vermin will also take eggs, so collect daily and keep tiny goslings penned.

If you have to cull a bird because of injury or illness, I would always contact the vet or an experienced breeder, because it's hard to explain how to dispatch humanely, better to be shown. Hopefully though, your geese will live long, happy and productive lives, providing you with plenty of entertainment, camaraderie and a lifetime membership of their flock.

Directory

Ducks and Geese at Home - M&V Roberts (Golden Cockerel)
Domestic Ducks and Geese - Fred Hams (Shire Publications)
Artificial Incubation & Rearing - J Batty (Beech Publishing)
The Book of Geese - Dave Holderread (Hen House Publications)

The Poultry Club of Gt. Britain	01205 724 081
The Domestic Waterfowl Club	01488 638 014
Allen & Page (Feed)	01362 822 900
The Domestic Fowl Trust Catalogue	01386 833 083
Intervits Equipment Catalogue	01142 552 340
Hugh Burton - Breeder Chinese Geese	01954 261 973
Gridfeed Thornber - Wire Pens	01706 815 131

The Kitchen Garden sells books and practical products by mail order or at the shop during the season and holds courses for poultry keepers and gardeners. Please phone for information 01359 268 322 or visit our website on www.kitchen-garden-hens.co.uk